★ ★ ★

PREDATOR DRONES

92-3034

BY JACK DAVID

BELLWETHER MEDIA · MINNEAPOLIS, MN

Are you ready to take it to the extreme?
Torque books thrust you into the action-packed
world of sports, vehicles, and adventure. These books
may include dirt, smoke, fire, and dangerous stunts.
WARNING: read at your own risk.

Library of Congress Cataloging-in-Publication Data

David, Jack, 1968-
  Predator drones / by Jack David.
      p. cm. -- (Torque, military machines)
  Summary: "Explains the technologies and capabilities of the latest generation of military Preda-
tor planes. Intended for grades 3 through 7 "--Provided by publisher.
  Includes bibliographical references and index.
  ISBN-13: 978-1-60014-105-8 (hbk. : alk. paper)
  ISBN-10: 1-60014-105-6 (hbk. : alk. paper)
  1. Predator (Drone aircraft)--Juvenile literature. I. Title. II. Series.

  UG1242.D7D38 2008
  623.74'67--dc22

                                                                              2007012162

CONTENTS

THE PREDATOR IN ACTION

A small unmanned plane called an MQ-1 Predator soars through the clouds. Its cameras take pictures of a hidden enemy base below.

★ **FAST FACT** ★

The Predator's radar can see in clouds, haze, fog, and smoke.

97-3034

WA

5

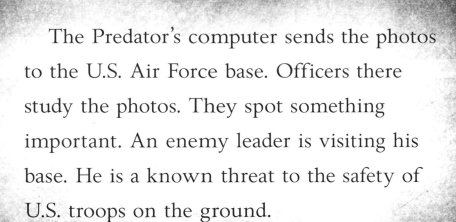

The Predator's computer sends the photos to the U.S. Air Force base. Officers there study the photos. They spot something important. An enemy leader is visiting his base. He is a known threat to the safety of U.S. troops on the ground.

The Predator is ready to complete its **mission**. The officers give the order: Fire! The Predator launches a single **missile**. An explosion flashes below. The enemy leader's truck is destroyed. The Predator's mission has been accomplished.

UNMANNED AERIAL VEHICLE

The Predator helps reduce risks for U.S. Air Force pilots. Enemies have shot down U.S. pilots on spy missions in the past. The Predator can accomplish spy missions without risking a pilot's life. It can also launch small attacks while spying.

★ **FAST FACT** ★

The Predator can remain airborne for more than 40 hours.

A pilot and sensor operator control the Predator.

The Predator is called a **drone** because it is
unmanned. The pilot and two **sensor operators**
remain on the ground and fly it by remote
control. Sensor operators work the plane's
cameras and sensors. They can fire the Predator's
missiles whenever a target is spotted.

SENSORS AND WEAPONS

The Predator's cameras and sensors gather information about the enemy. They allow the Predator to collect information during the night and during bad weather. All of this information helps the military plan attacks and prepare defenses.

A pilot cleans the sight lens.

★ **FAST FACT** ★

A Predator's engine produces only 101 horsepower. That is less than many motorcycles!

M-Q1 PREDATOR SPECIFICATIONS:

Primary Function: Unmanned aerial drone

Length: 27 feet (8 meters)

Height: 7 feet (2 meters)

Wingspan: 48.7 feet (15 meters)

Speed: 135 mph (217 km/h)

Range: 454 miles (731 kilometers)

Ceiling: 25,000 feet (7,620 meters)

Weight: 1,130 pounds (513 kilograms) empty

The Predator also carries attack weapons. Each drone can carry two AGM-114 Hellfire missiles. These small missiles are highly accurate. They are laser-guided. They're powerful enough to blast through thick tank **armor**.

PREDATOR MISSIONS

The Predator has performed very well in its missions. It has gathered important information about enemy groups. It has also carried out strikes against enemy leaders.

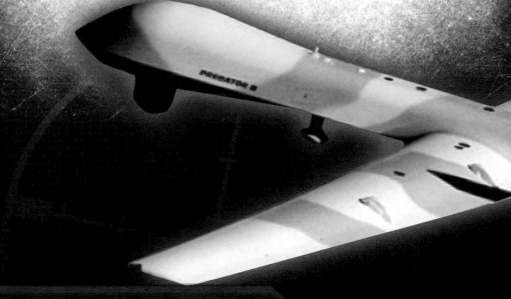

★ FAST FACT ★

Each Predator drone costs an estimated $4 million.

Crew members get ready for another mission.

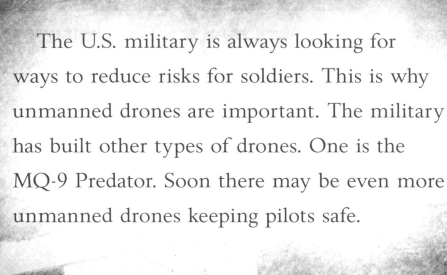

The U.S. military is always looking for ways to reduce risks for soldiers. This is why unmanned drones are important. The military has built other types of drones. One is the MQ-9 Predator. Soon there may be even more unmanned drones keeping pilots safe.

Crew members stay safe on the ground.

GLOSSARY

armor—protective plating

drone—an unmanned vehicle

missile—an explosive launched at targets on the ground or in the air

mission—a military task

sensor operator—a crew member who is in charge of a Predator's cameras and sensors

TO LEARN MORE

AT THE LIBRARY

Braulick, Carrie A. *U.S. Air Force Spy Planes*. Mankato, Minn.: Capstone Press, 2007.

Cooper, Jason. *U.S. Air Force*. Vero Beach, Fla.: Rourke, 2004.

Doeden, Matt. *The U.S. Air Force*. Mankato, Minn.: Capstone Press, 2005.

ON THE WEB

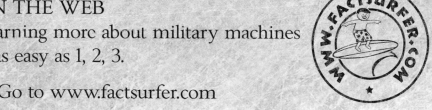

Learning more about military machines is as easy as 1, 2, 3.

1. Go to www.factsurfer.com

2. Enter "military machines" into search box.

3. Click the "Surf" button and you will see a list of related web sites.

With factsurfer.com, finding more information is just a click away.

INDEX